Empowered Parenting:

How to Manage Challenging Behaviour

Empowered Parenting: How to Manage Challenging Behaviour
© Copyright 2024 Maryna Repei
All rights reserved.

No part of this publication may be reproduced, distributed, or transmitted in any form or by any means, including photocopying, recording, or other electronic or mechanical methods, without prior written permission from the author.

ISBN: 9798334162952
Published by Maryna Repei
First Edition

Hello,

I'm Maryna, and I'm the mother of two wonderful children, one of whom is neurodiverse. My journey as a parent, along with my interest in child psychology and development, led me to pursue professional qualifications in mental health and learning disabilities. Through this journey, I've gained invaluable insights and strategies that have helped me support my children and benefit my family. I am passionate about sharing these insights and practical methods to help other parents navigate similar challenges using my personal experience and professional knowledge.

Parenting is a unique adventure, filled with joys and challenges. My greatest passion is understanding how children think, learn, and grow while creating a loving home where they can thrive. I believe every child has their own path to happiness, and it's our role as parents to nurture their individual skills and needs.

Beyond motherhood, I find joy in simple pleasures like traveling, finding peace by the sea, exploring new cuisines, and staying active through sports and exercise. These activities enrich my life and create a fulfilling environment for my children.

In "Empowered Parenting: How to Manage Challenging Behaviour," I share practical strategies, insights, and tips that have helped many parents, including myself. My goal is to empower parents to cultivate positive behaviour and create a supportive home environment for their children. Together, let's navigate challenges and celebrate the triumphs of raising happy, resilient kids.

Join me on this journey to help every child reach their full potential!

Contents

Chapter 1: Introduction   6
Importance and Goals of the Guide   6
How to Use This Guide for Maximum Benefit   7

Chapter 2: Understanding Child Behaviour   9
Developmental Milestones   10
Modern Insights and Practical Examples   13

Chapter 3: Identifying Behavioural Issues   20
Key Indicators of Problematic Behaviour   21
Practical Solutions for Addressing Behavioural Problems   23
Typical Behavioural Challenges at Various Stages of Childhood   30

Chapter 4: Understanding the Causes of Behaviour Problems   38
What Causes Behaviour Problems   38
Psychological Factors   42
Navigating Behavioural Challenges: Practical Tips and Real-Life Examples   45

Chapter 5: Recognising Neurodevelopmental Disorders   59
What are Neurodevelopmental Disorders?   59
Spotting Signs and Symptoms   61

Chapter 6: Positive Parenting Techniques   67
Encouraging Independence and Responsibility   67
Building Self-Esteem and Confidence   71
Dealing with Tantrums and Meltdowns   73

Chapter 7: Conclusion   82
Encouragement for Parents   82

Chapter 1
INTRODUCTION

Importance and Goals of the Guide

Welcome to a transformative parenting journey! This guide, "Empowered Parenting: How to Manage Challenging Behaviour", is a comprehensive tool-kit designed to provide you with effective strategies and insights to handle difficult behaviour in children. Whether you are dealing with tantrums, resistance, or simply want to improve your parenting abilities, this guide will help you understand and effectively shape your child's behaviour.

Parenting is a meaningful and fulfilling experience, but it also presents unique obstacles. This guide is designed to provide you with the knowledge and tools you need to confidently and clearly manage these obstacles. By digging into the complexity of child development, behavioural psychology, and effective communication tactics, you will discover the secrets to creating a happy home environment in which you and your child may thrive.

I know first-hand how exhausting it can be to deal with tantrums, stubbornness, and emotional outbursts. It's a difficult process that can leave you fatigued and stressed. But I'd like to remind you that you're not alone on this path. Every parent experiences difficult moments and questions their approach at times.

Throughout these pages, you'll find age-appropriate approaches and practical experience. From creating consistent routines and having clear expectations to using positive reinforcement and skilfully handling discipline, each chapter is designed to deliver actionable insights that you can put into action right away.

Our journey together begins with understanding: the stages of child development, the factors that influence behaviour, and the importance of your role as a parent. Armed with this knowledge, you'll be better able to adjust your approach to your child's specific requirements and challenges.

Most importantly, this guide serves as a reminder that parenting is about progress rather than perfection. Every day is an opportunity to learn and grow with your child. By implementing the ideas and practices outlined in this guide, you are taking proactive measures to create a caring, supportive environment in which your child can thrive emotionally, socially, and academically.

As you read this guide, you'll find practical suggestions that you can use right away to enhance your child's conduct and build family relationships. My goal is to present you with information that will help you improve your parenting skills.

Let us go on this adventure together, equipped with dedication and a steadfast determination to create a great future for your child.

How to Use This Guide for Maximum Benefit

To get the most out of this guide, start by familiarizing yourself with its structure and topics. As you read, consider how the thoughts and strategies will fit into your own parenting style.

Engage with the information by performing the suggested exercises or activities with your child. Don't be afraid to experiment and modify these

Chapter 1 | Introduction

tactics to fit your family dynamics and your child's personality. You'll learn what works best for your family by experimenting with different methods.

As you apply knowledge and tailor tactics to your child's needs, you will foster positive behaviour and strengthen your bond with them. Remember that it is not just about resolving urgent issues, but also about developing a stronger connection. Using these techniques properly will help you build a more positive relationship with your child.

This route is full of both challenges and successes. It's critical to appreciate tiny triumphs and acknowledge the strength you demonstrate every day. I hope this guide provides you with practical strategies and reassures you of the value of your dedication. You're doing an amazing job, and your love and patience are important tools for helping your child develop. Together, we can overcome these challenges and create a supportive atmosphere in which you and your child can thrive.

Chapter 2
UNDERSTANDING CHILD BEHAVIOUR

Attempting to forecast the weather in a tropical rainforest is like trying to understand why a child's behaviour is always changing — completely unpredictable and full of surprises! Young children are insatiably inquisitive, exploring their environment through play and experimentation. Suddenly, they transform from sweet angels sharing cookies into whirling little tornadoes tearing up your living room. Parents can create environments that promote resilience, independence, and happiness by understanding the unique dynamics of each child's journey.

Trying to make sense of how children act is like setting out on an exciting adventure where you get to learn something new at every turn. Have you ever stopped to consider, "What was my child's funniest moment today that I'll be laughing about even now?" Or thought, "How can I turn today's challenges into tomorrow's victories?"

As parents, the most important thing we can do to support our child's growth is to welcome these changes and successes as they occur. To help you understand your child, ask yourself, "What makes my child unique?" and "How can I cheer them on in their journey?"

Every child's journey is unique, packed with unexpected twists and charming quirks. Recognising the distinct developmental milestones and difficulties children encounter at different life stages is critical to understanding child behaviour. The best way for parents to help their children develop, encourage positive habits, and form trustworthy relationships is to use current research and tried-and-true methods. The next time you're puzzled, ask yourself, "What little thing can I do today to support my child's development and joy?"

Chapter 2 | Understanding Child Behaviour

Developmental Milestones

Infancy (0-1 year)

Infancy is a time of fast growth and building strong foundations:

- **Motor Development:** To help build muscles and support early motor skills, encourage tummy time, which involves lying on one's stomach while awake, and create safe areas for exploration.

- **Social and Emotional Development:** Establish trust and emotional safety by quickly responding to the baby's signals, like cries or coos.

Examples:

- A baby's smile in reaction to a parent's face shows early social connection and emotional attentiveness.

- Using peek-a-boo activities, mirror play, and singing songs to boost social contact and bonding.

- Using baby sign language can improve communication and reduce frustration before spoken skills mature fully.

Young children (1–5 years old)

There are important cognitive and social-emotional stages in early childhood:

- **Language and Communication:** To improve your language and vocabulary, have talks, ask open-ended questions, and listen carefully.

- **Cognitive Development:** Give them books, games, and puzzles that are suitable for their age to help them think critically and solve problems.

- **Social Skills:** Plan play dates and group events to help kids learn how to share, wait their turn, and work together with others.

Examples:

- Reading with expressive intonation improves language comprehension and storytelling skills.

- During playtime, teach sharing and turn-taking skills through structured games, such as building blocks or board games.

- Creating a visual daily routine chart with pictures can help children comprehend and anticipate everyday routines, leading to increased independence and reduced anxiety.

Middle Childhood (6–12 years)

Middle childhood emphasizes developing cognitive skills, social contacts, and emotional resilience:

- **Cognitive Skills:** Use science experiments, art activities, and other hands-on tasks to spark your child's interest in learning and exploration.

- **Social Development:** Teach conflict resolution and kindness to help kids build friendships and relationships with their peers.

- **Emotional Regulation:** To help children deal with stress and emotions well, teach them deep breathing exercises and mindfulness methods.

Examples:

- Encouraging a child to do research for and carry out a simple science project at home, which builds their interest and ability to think critically.

- Playing pretend helps kids see things from different points of view and learn to understand how others feel.

- Setting up a "worry box" where kids can write down and talk to their parents about their worries and concerns, encouraging open conversation and emotional expression.

Teenage years (13–18 years)

Teenage years are a time of change when bodies change, identities are formed, and freedom grows:

- **Physical Growth:** To improve overall health and self-confidence, encourage regular physical exercise and healthy eating habits.

- **Identity Exploration:** Give kids opportunities to learn more about their interests and passions by providing them with hobbies, extracurricular activities, and volunteer work.

- **Social Influences:** To help children make smart choices, talk about group pressure, how to behave on social media, and how to stay safe online.

Examples:

- Helping a teen do community service is a way to learn more about their own values and hobbies.

- Talking with your family about how to deal with social pressures and how your friends connect with each other over meals.

- Setting up parental controls and talking about digital behaviour to make sure kids use technology safely and responsibly, and to make sure they don't spend too much time in front of the screen.

Modern Insights and Practical Examples

Maintaining harmony between online and offline activities is similar to juggling: you're continuously striving to keep everything in the air without dropping the ball. Consider the following questions: "How much screen time is my child getting daily?" Additionally, "What offline activities can we enjoy together?" Think about this: "How can we make offline activities as exciting as their favourite online game?"

Remember that the goal is to identify what works best for your family. And don't worry if some days are more balanced than others; every attempt counts! What about setting a screen time limit? Think of it like a microwave timer: once the timer goes off, it's over! How about including your child in creating a list of fun offline activities? In this way, children become enthused about the options and feel included in the decision-making process.

In today's digital world, keeping a good balance between screen time and offline activities is critical for children's well-being:

- ✓ **Setting Limits:** Make clear rules about computer time based on what's best for your child's age and your family's values.

- ✓ **Good Content:** Support educational apps, games that you can interact with, and media that is proper for your child's age that helps them learn and be creative.

- ✓ **Family Engagement:** Set aside times without devices, like family dinners or events outside, to talk to each other and bond in person.

Examples:

- Creating a "technology basket" in which all family members stow their gadgets during scheduled family time to encourage uninterrupted connection and conversation.

- Establishing a family technology agreement that outlines screen time guidelines and expectations for appropriate device use.

- Using educational applications and interactive media to engage children in learning activities that are appropriate for their interests and developmental stage.

Positive Discipline Techniques

Positive discipline is mentoring your child with respect and encouragement rather than punishment. Think to yourself, "What do I do when my child tests my patience?" Consider asking yourself, "What's a good way for me to deal with bad behaviour?" Having fun also helps! You could say something like, "Wow, I see you're going for the Picasso look!" when you catch your little artist at work instead of yelling. Could we use paper

Chapter 2 | Understanding Child Behaviour

instead?" It transforms a situation that could be stressful into a chance to learn.

> It is important to teach and guide children toward responsible behaviour through constructive discipline, which uses praise and rewards:

✓ **Positive reinforcement:** Praise effort and success to support good habits such as finishing tasks, doing housework, or treating siblings with kindness.

✓ **Consistency:** Clearly state what is expected of you and what will happen if you don't follow through. This will make things fair and predictable.

✓ **Problem-Solving:** To help kids think critically and take responsibility, let them come up with creative answers to problems or conflicts.

One other thing: make sure the rules are clear and always follow them. Children thrive on routine and knowing what to expect. Have you ever created a fun, colourful chart outlining rules and rewards? It's like turning your household into a game in which obeying the rules results in favourable outcomes. What rules can you establish that are clear and consistent?

Examples:

- Creating a chart that kids may use to collect stars or tokens for doing good deeds and tasks; the goal is to save up for a special family activity or outing.

15

- Teaching methods for resolving conflicts and solving problems through the use of role-playing activities.

- Making sure everyone in the family understands and works together by talking about the rules and punishments.

Cultivating Emotional Intelligence

Have you ever found it puzzling that your child's feelings seem to change faster than the temperature outside? Raising emotional intelligence in your children will enable them to negotiate this roller-coaster. How then can we achieve this without losing our sanity?

Starting with encouraging your child to express feelings through journalling, music, or art is great. Ever tried sketching your emotions? Though it seems a bit ridiculous, it's quite powerful. Imagine asking your child, "What colour is your anger today?" It's not only artistic; it's also a light-hearted approach for kids to help sort their feelings.

How could humour help to defuse difficult circumstances? When your child is about to lose it, try to soften the situation. "Hey, did you know that even superheroes have terrible days? What do you suppose Spider-Man does when he gets annoyed?" This can make a possible outburst a teaching tool for emotional regulation.

So, the next time emotions run strong, inhale deeply, laugh, and keep in mind — you've got this!

> Emotional intelligence is essential for dealing with feelings, becoming more resilient, and making good connections with others:

- ✓ **Emotion Coaching:** Validate and name emotions to help kids understand and deal with them better.

- ✓ **Building empathy:** Use stories or role-playing games to help people see things from other people's points of view and understand how they feel.

- ✓ **Self-Care:** Teach skills for relaxing yourself, like deep breathing or writing in a journal, to help you control your emotions and feel good.

Examples:

- Making a "feelings jar" with emotion cards for children to select and discuss, so encouraging self-awareness and emotional expressiveness.

- Modelling healthy coping methods, such as taking a break or using calming techniques, during moments of stress or anger.

- Encouraging children to express themselves and release emotions through art, music, or journalling.

Engaging in Creative Pursuits

Have you ever tried painting with your child and ended up with more paint on you than on the canvas? You share more than just art; it's about the enjoyment and connection you have. Have you seen how your child can use imagination to turn a plain cardboard box into a castle or a comet? Their creativity is endless!

Consider: How often do you participate in these creative activities with your child? What have you learned about them from their pictures or music? Remember, it's not about being the next Picasso; it's about the process and the enjoyment it offers.

Engaging children in creative activities such as art, music, and journalling is beneficial to their emotional and cognitive development. These activities provide a secure place for children to express complicated feelings that they may struggle to articulate. When children paint, make music, or write in a journal, they learn important emotional regulation and self-expression skills, both of which are necessary for optimal mental health.

As parents, participating in these creative excursions not only enhances your bond with your child, but also demonstrates your support for their emotional journey. Imagine sitting down at the kitchen table and drawing humorous characters or writing songs about everyday events. This would give them a chance to get to know each other better while also encouraging their creativity.

Furthermore, creative pursuits inspire in children self-awareness and contemplation. Children explore their ideas and experiences through art or journal writing, thereby illuminating their own feelings and actions. Through this contemplation, children develop both personally and socially, enhancing their capacity to negotiate friendships and understand several points of view.

Children who engage in creative pursuits also develop resilience. Dealing with artistic obstacles or experimenting with new approaches teaches endurance and problem-solving ability. These encounters help adolescents see losses as opportunities for personal development, empowering them to confidently meet the demands of life.

Therefore, the next time you're thinking about how to improve your child's growth, consider getting some paintbrushes, grabbing musical instruments, or encouraging them to journal. Along with helping children to be creative, you will be supporting their emotional well-being and getting them ready for a great future.

Chapter 3
IDENTIFYING BEHAVIOURAL ISSUES

As children grow, they exhibit a variety of behaviours, many of which are natural stages of development. Understanding when a child's behaviour is inappropriate can be difficult for parents. Misbehaviours are not always indicative of deeper concerns; they can sometimes be a normal part of growing up. However, recognising the signs and symptoms of behavioural issues is critical for timely intervention and assistance.

Managing behavioural issues in children may be extremely difficult and demanding. Tantrums, resistance, and emotional outbursts are difficult to deal with on a daily basis. The ongoing effort to maintain consistency, enforce regulations, and offer emotional support can leave parents exhausted and stressed. Balancing the responsibilities of home life with your child's behavioural requirements might be difficult at times. However, knowing that these difficulties are common in parenting and that there are effective coping skills will help you remain resilient and hopeful.

I'd like to take a moment to highlight the enormous challenges that come with managing problematic child behaviour. Because I am a mum myself, I realize how difficult it is. There are days when it feels like an uphill battle, and the demands of family life may seem insurmountable. However, please keep in mind that your efforts do have an impact.

Every time you set boundaries, provide a reassuring embrace, support your child's efforts, celebrate their accomplishments, or simply listen to them, you contribute to their development and well-being. Every parent experiences difficult moments and questions their approach at times. You are not alone on this path. Your dedication is important, and together

Chapter 3 | Identifying Behavioural Issues

we can overcome these hurdles to create a caring atmosphere in which both you and your child can thrive.

Key Indicators of Problematic Behaviour

It might feel like detective work in order to figure out if your child's behaviour is just a phase or a sign of something more serious, right? Every child acts out at times — it's as if they're training for a Broadway production called "Growing Up!". But when should you start thinking, "Hmm, maybe we should talk to an expert?"

Behavioural problems can manifest in a variety of ways, and by correctly diagnosing these symptoms, parents can address underlying issues early on, assisting their children in developing healthier coping skills and building a more pleasant home atmosphere. Keep an eye out for patterns. Is it just a terrible day now and again, or is it an ongoing roller-coaster ride?

Remember that every child is unique, like a puzzle with no instructions. What works for one person may not work for another, which is just fine! You're not alone in this — imagine all the parents out there, turning through life's parenting manual, looking for the appropriate chapter. So, take a deep breath, trust yourself, and know that with a little detective work and counsel, you'll have this parenting gig covered!

Key indicators that can be used for early intervention and support:

- **Frequent tantrums and aggression:** Having the odd temper tantrum is normal, but hitting, biting, kicking, or other violent outbursts that happen often may be a sign of deeper problems. For example, a child who always acts out when they're upset about small things could have more than one phase.

Chapter 3 | Identifying Behavioural Issues

- **Persistent Disobedience:** While all children challenge limits, a child may have a more underlying problem if they regularly disobey directions and regulations despite continuous discipline. A child who consistently refuses to complete homework or chores despite rewards, for example, might require more help.

- **Social Withdrawal:** If a child avoids social events on a regular basis, has trouble making friends, or seems extra nervous around other people, they may be having social or emotional issues. For example, a child who likes to play alone and gets upset when asked to do things with other kids might need help.

- **Too Much Fear Or Anxiety:** Some fear and anxiety are normal, but thoughts that are too strong or don't make sense and get in the way of daily life can be scary. For example, a child who dreads going to school even though it's a safe place to be could be dealing with serious anxiety and needs help.

- **Difficulties Concentrating:** Attention and focus issues that get in the way of learning or social interactions could be signs of a condition like ADHD. For instance, a child who gets sidetracked easily, forgets things, and has trouble following directions might benefit from more testing and help.

Early detection of these symptoms and appropriate assistance can help address underlying problems and promote the child's development and well-being.

Chapter 3 | Identifying Behavioural Issues

Practical Solutions for Addressing Behavioural Problems

In our individual ways, every parent acts as a detective when attempting to understand their child's actions. Understanding what is typical and what may require further attention is like reading their behaviour between the lines.

When trying to identify when something is harmful, it is important to consider the frequency, length, and impact of the behaviour. A child who tantrums occasionally is different from one who does so daily. Temporary stresses may cause short-term shifts, but more serious problems may require long-term action. When these behaviours become more frequent or severe or start to affect their daily lives, such as school problems or long-term sadness, they may need to stop and pay attention. As a parent, you should trust your instincts; you know your child best. Disruptions to home life, academic performance, or social connections raise red flags.

It is perfectly acceptable to consult with experts or trusted friends and family. Seeking help for your child's mental health is like taking your car in for routine maintenance; it's all about making sure they have what they need to succeed. You can help your child face life's obstacles with confidence if you pay close attention to their actions and feelings.

> The most useful ways to deal with behaviour issues are those that are based on facts and focus on making the surroundings positive, organised, and helpful. Here are five of these approaches, along with reasons why they work:

1. Giving praise and rewards

Using rewards to motivate the repetition of good behaviour is one way to do this. Rewards can be verbal praise, tokens, privileges, or tangible items.

> **Why it helps:** Positive reinforcement helps kids know what actions are wanted and appreciated. It encourages them to behave well because they connect it with positive things happening, which boosts their self-esteem and makes the relationship between parent and child better.

2. Making rules that are clear and consistent

Clearly communicating and following your expectations helps kids understand boundaries.

> **Why it helps:** Consistent rules give children structure and predictability, which makes them less anxious and confused about what is and isn't okay to do. Kids are more likely to behave properly when they know what will happen if they don't.

3. Effective Communication

Addressing the causes of behaviour problems begins with active listening and honest, open communication.

Chapter 3 | Identifying Behavioural Issues

Why it helps: Kids are more likely to talk about their feelings and work together if they feel like they are being heard and understood. Good communication helps people trust each other and figure out what problems may be going on underneath their behaviour.

4. Time-Outs and Cool-Down Periods

A time-out removes a child from an environment where they are acting out, allowing them to calm down and reflect on their actions.

Why it helps: Time-outs give the child a break from the things that might be making them act out. They teach kids how to control themselves, as well as what will happen if they do something wrong in a calm and controlled way.

5. Emotion Regulation Techniques

Assist kids in controlling their feelings by teaching them specific methods like deep breathing, counting to ten, or using a calm-down area.

Why it helps: Emotion regulation methods teach kids healthy ways to deal with their anger and frustration. This can reduce the frequency and severity of angry outbursts and temper tantrums. Teaching these skills gives kids the power to handle their feelings and act more calmly in stressful scenarios.

Chapter 3 | Identifying Behavioural Issues

Ever wondered how to help your child manage their big emotions? Teaching children to manage those big feelings isn't just about preventing meltdowns — it's setting them up for a happier, more resilient future! Picture it as giving them a tool-kit for life, equipped with skills to handle stress and bounce back from challenges. So, how can you sprinkle some emotion-regulating magic into your daily routines? Here are five practical techniques to help your kids master their emotions:

- **Journalling or Drawing**

Encouraging children to express their feelings through journalling or drawing gives them a constructive outlet for their emotions. Journalling organises thoughts, while drawing benefits younger children who can't yet articulate their feelings. Both activities enhance emotional awareness and communication skills.

- **Progressive Muscle Relaxation**

Progressive muscle relaxation (PMR) involves tensing and relaxing muscle groups, helping children recognise and release physical tension. PMR reduces stress and anxiety, promoting a sense of calm and better sleep. This technique empowers children to manage their stress responses.

- **Using a Calm-Down Corner**

A calm-down corner is a safe space with comforting items that children can retreat to when overwhelmed. It provides a structured environment for regaining composure and developing effective coping strategies. Regular use teaches children to recognise and manage stress independently.

- **Physical Activity**

Physical activity helps children release energy, manage emotions, reduce stress, and improve mood through endorphins. Activities like running, dancing, or sports enhance focus, coordination, and physical health, leading to better emotional balance. Yoga and stretching promote relaxation and mindfulness. Regular exercise builds resilience and healthy coping mechanisms.

- **Deep Breathing**

Deep breathing exercises help children slow down their breathing and calm their nervous system. Techniques such as belly breathing or the 4-7-8 method can help to reduce stress and anxiety quickly. Deep breathing increases oxygen flow to the brain, promoting relaxation and clarity of thought. It's a simple yet powerful tool that children can use anytime they feel overwhelmed.

Life Example 1: Persistent Aggression

Liam, who is seven years old, often hits his friends and throws things when he is irritated or upset. Even though his parents and teachers try to control his behaviour, the violence keeps getting worse, which worries adults. Even though his parents and teachers try to control his behaviour, the violence keeps getting worse, which worries adults.

What was done: At home, Liam's parents use an organized behaviour plan that makes it clear what they expect from him and what will happen if he acts aggressively. They show Liam other ways to deal with his anger, like deep breathing routines or finding a quiet place to take a break. Additionally, Liam's parents often encourage him to express his thoughts instead of acting out. With constant direction and positive reinforcement, Liam gradually learns to control his anger and temper.

Life Example 2: Intense Tantrums

Five-year-old Emma has violent tantrums many times a day that last longer than thirty minutes. These outbursts, which can occur at home or in public, involve beating, kicking, and yelling.

What was done: Emma's parents begin monitoring triggers and patterns of her behaviour by maintaining a behaviour notebook. To provide stability, they establish a regular daily schedule that includes set meal times, supervised playtime, and bedtime routines. Emma's parents set up positive reinforcement techniques such as stickers, charts, and awards for excellent behaviour. They also use positive feedback, telling her how proud they are that she can talk about her feelings instead of throwing fits. Emma learns to better control her emotions with her parents' help, and as a result, her tantrums become less frequent and intense over time.

Life Example 3: Social Withdrawal

Ten-year-old James withdraws from society more and more. He doesn't want to do the things he used to enjoy and would rather stay in his room. His school work also gets much worse.

What was done: James' parents start talking to him openly to find out how he feels and what worries him. They make it possible for James to do things he likes at home and encourage him to be a part of small groups with close family or friends. His parents provide mental support and reassurance by consistently praising positive behaviour and celebrating small successes. With their help and understanding, James slowly starts to feel more at ease with making friends and getting back in touch with people outside of his close family.

Life Example 4: Disruptive Behaviour at School

Sofia, who is twelve years old, often talks back to her teacher, disrupts class, and refuses to do her chores. Her negative behaviour gets worse despite disciplinary sanctions, which impacts her academic performance and her relationships with peers.

What was done: Sofia's parents and teachers work closely together to deal with her behaviour. At home, they set up a pattern with clear rules, consistent consequences for positive and undesirable behaviour, and clear standards. They talk openly with Sofia about her problems and feelings, and they offer support and motivation to help her do well. They also enrol Sofia in extracurricular activities that align with her hobbies. This gives her healthy ways to use her energy and creativity. Through continued parental advice and school support, Sofia's behaviour and academic performance start to get better, making the classroom a better place for her and her peers to learn.

Life Example 5: Disruptive Behaviour at Home

Nine-year-old Emily regularly acts disruptively at home. She fights with her siblings, defies house rules, and acts out when asked to finish homework or housework. Her inappropriate behaviour disrupts family dinners and generates disagreements during trips, stressing the family.

What was done: Emily's parents have a set daily schedule, including specific times for family events, homework, and housework. They design a chore chart with well-defined expectations and implement a reward system where Emily gets privileges or special activities for demonstrating positive behaviour. For disruptive behaviour, Emily's parents also set regular penalties, such as screen time or privileges lost. They initiate honest conversations with Emily in quiet times to learn about her feelings and difficulties, thereby providing emotional support and direction. Emily's behaviour gets better with regular schedules, well-defined rules, and encouraging words. She gains greater control of her feelings, follows guidelines with less effort, and participates actively in family events. This improves the harmony in her house and develops her bonds with her relatives.

Typical Behavioural Challenges at Various Stages of Childhood

Understanding typical behavioural issues among different age groups can help parents support their children's successful growth as their behaviour changes as they mature. Being aware of these problems early on and dealing with them in the right way can make a big difference.

Infancy and Toddler-hood (0-3 years)

Behavioural Problems:

- **Temper tantrums:** Toddlers often throw temper tantrums because they find it difficult to say what they want and are upset about it. These strong emotional outbursts can be hard, but they are a normal part of growing up.

- **Separation Anxiety:** Babies and children often get upset when they are taken away from their family members. This can manifest as crying, a need for physical touch, or a reluctance to leave them with others.

Life Examples

Example 1: Sarah, who was two years old, frequently threw tantrums in the grocery store. Her parents knew that she usually threw these fits when she was hungry or tired. They greatly decreased her temper tantrums by planning shopping trips for after her nap and bringing snacks with them.

Example 2: Ethan, a three-year-old boy, had a hard time being dropped off at daycare. "Goodbye routine" for his mum included a special hug and a promise to see him soon. This steady pattern made Ethan feel safer, and over time, his worry about being alone got better.

Practical Tips:

✓ To keep temper tantrums to a minimum, set up habits that your child can count on and be aware of what might set them off, such as being hungry or tired.

✓ Make sure you always say goodbye, or implement a kind goodbye routine with hugs to bring comfort when you have to go your separate ways. This will help you feel safe and comforted.

Chapter 3 | Identifying Behavioural Issues

✓ Gradually give your child more freedom, letting them learn how to handle being alone and their feelings while building their confidence.

Early Childhood (3-6 years)

Behavioural Problems:

- **Defiance:** Frequent "no" and boundary testing help children in this age range establish their independence.

- **Social Problems:** As children learn how to get along with others, they often have trouble sharing, waiting for their turn, and working together.

Life Examples

Example 1: Mia, a four-year-old, often wouldn't do what her parents told her to do at home and would say "no" to everything they asked. To fix this, Mia's parents set up a reward plan where she could get stickers for every job she did without complaining. This positive feedback made Mia more likely to follow the rules every time.

Example 2: Leo, a five-year-old, had a difficult time sharing toys at preschool and would get irritated when he had to wait his turn. During playtime, Leo's teacher set up role-playing games so that the kids could practice sharing things and waiting their turn. These skills helped Leo work together better with his friends over time.

Chapter 3 | Identifying Behavioural Issues

Practical Tips:

✓ Apply positive reinforcement by setting up sticker systems or reward charts to inspire home rule compliance and collaboration.

✓ Be Clear About Expectations: Make rules and expectations for behaviour very clear, and always back them up with praise and other positive feedback when kids follow them.

✓ Role-Playing Social Scenarios: Play role-taking games with your kids that make them feel like they are sharing, waiting their turn, and other social situations they might face. This hands-on method gives them a safe place to learn and practice these skills.

Middle Childhood (6-12 years)

Behavioural Problems:

- **Difficulty Paying Attention:** Children in this age range may have trouble concentrating, which might affect their academic achievement.

- **Peer Pressure:** Managing friends and their pressures can lead to behavioural changes and difficulties.

- **Disobedience and Resistance:** Children often conflict with adults, simply refuse to abide by the rules, or intentionally upset those around them.

Chapter 3 | Identifying Behavioural Issues

Life Examples

Example 1: Olivia, who was eight years old, struggled to pay attention in class and finish her assignments. Following consultations with her physician and teacher, Olivia's parents created a peaceful homework schedule and made use of a timer to facilitate her concentration at brief intervals. After implementing this methodical approach, her focus was more prolonged.

Example 2: Noah, who is ten years old, started acting out and not doing his chores to fit in with a new group of friends. Because they were worried, his parents talked to him openly about group pressure and what happens when you give in. They suggested Noah join a sports team, where he made good friends and got back on track with his studies, which made him behave better at school and at home.

Practical Tips:

✓ To increase attention span, set up a disciplined, calm homework routine, including periods for relaxation or physical exercise.

✓ Talk to your child often about the dangers of peer pressure and the significance of making positive decisions.

✓ Get children involved in activities outside of school, such as sports or interest clubs, to help them make good friends and behave well.

Chapter 3 | Identifying Behavioural Issues

Adolescence (13-18 years)

Behavioural Problems:

- **Taking risks:** As teenagers try to find their freedom and figure out who they are, they often do dangerous things.

- **Emotional Chaos:** The teenage years are a time of big changes in emotions, which can cause mood swings and fights with family members.

- **Academic Stress:** Anxiety, procrastination, and even avoidance behaviours can result from pressure to perform well in the classroom.

- **Social Pressure:** Teenagers may feel pressured by others to fit in, which could lead to negative habits such as substance misuse or improper use of social media.

Life Examples

Example 1: Staying out late without telling her parents was one of Emily's dangerous behaviours when she was fourteen years old. Emily learned the value of trust and safety in the family through honest dialogue and the establishment of clear boundaries.

Example 2: Fifteen-year-old Alex frequently went through mood swings and got into conflicts with his parents. They improved their connection and emotional understanding by attending family therapy sessions, where they learned practical communication techniques and conflict resolution techniques.

Chapter 3 | Identifying Behavioural Issues

Practical Tips:

✓ Encourage an open conversation by listening to your teenager's concerns and giving them advice without passing judgment.

✓ When things are tough, think about family therapy to help everyone talk to each other and understand each other better.

✓ Make sure your child knows what the rules are so they can make beneficial decisions while staying safe and healthy.

Distraction can be like a cool breeze in a stuffy room when emotions boil and tensions increase. It's about gently moving your child's attention away from the heat of the moment, not about discounting the problem. Imagine it as guiding the flow of a river — it alters its momentum toward a calmer direction but not its course.

Adopting distraction teaches emotional control and resilience in addition to helping you to avoid conflict. Children who possess this talent will be able to gracefully and adaptably negotiate the obstacles of life into maturity. Therefore, keep in mind the power of distraction — it's not only a parenting trick but also a deep approach to promoting development and comprehension in your child — regardless of the quick surge of irritation or a furious quarrel over toys.

Knowing typical behavioural issues across several ages can be like negotiating a maze. Though every turn offers fresh difficulties, knowing what to expect guides you. Consider: "What amusing story will I be able to tell?"

Similar to putting seeds in a garden, identifying and resolving behavioural disorders at an early stage is crucial. If you take the right steps, your work will pay off, but it might not happen right away. You might want to ask yourself, "What small steps can I take to make a difference?" "How can I support my child's well-being today?"

With understanding and patience, you can help your child overcome the challenges that come with each developmental stage. Your love and support, together with practice help when necessary, can greatly impact your child's happiness and development; just keep in mind that every child's journey is unique. Ask yourself, "What's one thing I'm proud of today, no matter how small?" and take a deep breath when you're feeling overwhelmed.

Being there for your child emotionally can help them develop emotional intelligence and self-control. Think, "How can I be a source of comfort for my child today?" This means that your child is better able to deal with both positive and negative feelings. Think, "What can I do to create a sense of security and stability at home?"

A child's sense of safety and stability increases when they have emotional support at home. Take into account, "How do my presence and understanding boost my child's confidence?" As a result, their mental and emotional well-being increases, and they acquire the resilience needed to handle life's unavoidable obstacles with dignity and grace.

Knowing that you're available to listen and understand will boost your child's self-esteem. Consider, "What small gestures can show my child I'm here for them?" The mental support you give them is what helps them grow into strong, self-confident people.

Chapter 4
UNDERSTANDING THE CAUSES OF BEHAVIOUR PROBLEMS

What Causes Behaviour Problems

It's normal to feel disappointed, helpless, and overwhelmed when you don't understand your child's intentions. The unexpected outbursts, the ongoing fights over insignificant matters, and the anxiety about whether we're doing things right may be burdensome. Feeling overwhelmed is not a sign of failure. Instead, it shows how much you care about your child's growth and health.

To get through these tough times, you need to know why your child is acting the way they are. Understanding what makes them act out, whether it's emotional problems, stages of growth, or outside factors, gives you the power to react in a beneficial way. Take small steps on a daily basis to learn what your child needs and how to help them.

If parents want to respond appropriately and compassionately to their child's needs, they must first understand what is causing their child's behavioural difficulties. To respond appropriately, parents must first identify the emotions and thoughts that cause their children to act out, be it anger, worry, or a need for attention. Becoming aware of these reasons can help you grow in a beneficial way. Parental care and support can improve behavioural challenges by addressing the root causes, which may include social problems, developmental issues, or environmental stresses. This method helps kids deal with problems right away and builds their mental health and endurance at the same time.

Chapter 4 | Understanding the Causes of Behaviour Problems

Understanding the causes of behaviour is crucial for early intervention. Early detection and treatment can prevent problems from worsening or becoming entrenched. And now you should ask yourself, "What small steps can I take today to better understand how my child acts?" How can I change the way I do things to meet their specific needs? Early assistance can make a huge difference in a child's development, whether it means getting professional help for developmental issues or changing the way you parent to better meet the child's needs.

Knowing why a child is acting up also strengthens the bond between parent and child and encourages making strong connections. When parents respond with understanding and help instead of anger or punishment, it strengthens connections and trust. Take a moment to reflect on a recent event where you demonstrated kindness instead of reacting without thought. What changes did it make in your relationship with your child? This positive contact sets the stage for healthy mental growth and makes the bond between parent and child stronger.

Lastly, every child is different, and parents can help their kids in the best way possible by knowing the specific things that affect their behaviour. Personalized support helps kids do well and reach their full potential, whether it's by changing routines, teaching them how to deal with problems, or getting expert help for underlying conditions.

Effective parenting depends on understanding the underlying reasons for children's behaviour issues. In this conversation, the emphasis is on exploring the several elements influencing children's behaviour and offering ideas to help solve these problems:

Chapter 4 | Understanding the Causes of Behaviour Problems

Developmental Factors

Children vary significantly in their development, which affects their behaviour. As they learn to express their needs and feelings, toddlers, for instance, sometimes struggle with outbursts. As children start to express their independence and struggle with fresh emotions, these outbursts are a natural aspect of their growth stage.

> **Example:** When three-year-old Sarah can't find the right words to describe how she feels, she often has tantrums. She expresses her increasing independence and copes with frustration through these emotional outbursts.

Environmental Factors

A child's upbringing, particularly their home and school conditions, greatly influences how they act. Some of the things that might affect a child's behaviour include difficult family relationships, irregular routines, and big life events like moving.

> **Example:** Alex, a seven-year-old, started acting out at school after relocating to a new city. Moving the house disrupted his sense of safety and regularity, triggering his anxiety and outbursts.

Emotional and Social Factors

A child's emotional health and the quality of their social relationships have a significant impact on their conduct. Behavioural issues might be a symptom of deeper issues like bullying, insecurity, or pressure from peers.

> **Example:** After being the target of bullying at school, six-year-old Mia began to exhibit symptoms of anxiety and withdrawal. As she battled to overcome the psychological effects of bullying, her behaviour at home became increasingly problematic.

Parenting Style

A parent's interaction style has a major effect on their children's behaviour. Positive behaviour is more likely to flourish under authoritative parenting styles that blend warmth with firm limits. On the other side, behavioural problems may stem from either authoritarian or too lenient parenting.

> **Example:** Ethan's behaviour improved when his parents used a consistent approach to sanction and gave rewards for excellent behaviour. This method enabled Ethan to feel supported and appreciated while also understanding limits.

Biological Factors

Disorders of sensory processing, attention deficit hyperactivity disorder (ADHD), or autism spectrum disorder (ASD) may arise as underlying

Chapter 4 | Understanding the Causes of Behaviour Problems

causes of some behavioural abnormalities. Early detection of these problems can lead to better care and solutions.

> **Example:** Nine-year-old James struggled to keep his concentration while doing homework in the classroom. Following an exhaustive assessment, he received an ADHD diagnosis. James chose techniques to control his concentration problems and improve his school behaviour with the correct help from parents and instructors.

Psychological Factors

Children's behaviour can be influenced by a variety of psychological factors, including their thoughts, feelings, and responses to their surroundings. Like a child with a toy box full of opportunities, their small minds seem to be juggling emotions, ideas, and reactions in search of the ideal state of balance. These psychological factors include:

Emotional Regulation

This relates to a child's capacity to control and appropriately communicate their emotions. Frustration, disappointment, and anxiousness are among the emotions that children who have trouble controlling their emotions may find challenging to deal with.

> **Example:** Young children who act out when informed they cannot get a preferred toy at the store are showing poor emotional control. Another scenario could be a child who, unable to control their fear of failing, starts to withdraw or gets very nervous before a test at school.

Chapter 4 | Understanding the Causes of Behaviour Problems

Temperament

A child's temperament is made up of the natural traits that affect how they respond to things that stress them out or stimulate them in their surroundings. When children have different personalities, they might react to the same situation in different ways.

> **Example:** Kids with a highly emotional personality might get scared or upset by loud noises or changes in their routine, which could make them act out by crying or getting angry. On the other hand, a child with a more laid-back personality might be able to handle these changes with less stress.

Cognitive Challenges

Cognitive challenges, including learning difficulties, processing problems, or deficits in executive functioning, can have an immense impact on behaviour.

> **Example:** Children with ADHD may struggle with hyperactivity, impulsiveness, and attention span maintenance. In a classroom, this might manifest as regular disruptions during a lesson or difficulty staying focused on assignments.

Past Events and Trauma

Children who have been through trauma, abuse, or neglect may have behaviour problems because their feelings and ways of dealing aren't fully settled.

> **Example:** If a child has seen domestic abuse, they might act aggressively to protect themselves or take charge when things go wrong. Consider a child who has experienced a significant loss, such as death of a close person, and now acts sad or withdraws from others.

Family Dynamics and Parenting Styles

A child's behaviour is greatly affected by the way their parents raise them and the way their family functions.

> **Example:** Inconsistent punishment, insufficient positive feedback, or harsh parenting can lead to behaviour problems. On the other hand, adaptive behaviours and mental control are more likely to happen when parents are strict, set clear goals, and use positive feedback.

Social and Peer Influences

In childhood and adolescence, interactions and peer connections can shape behaviour.

> **Example:** Children struggling with social skills or experiencing

peer bullying may resort to acting out as a coping mechanism or a means of fitting in. Consider the possibility of a school-teasing child shutting down or feeling nervous, leading to a change in their behaviour both inside and outside of school.

Knowing these psychological factors enables parents and other caregivers to identify the fundamental reasons for children's behavioural issues. It helps people get to the core of what's happening rather than only seeing the surface of outbursts or mood swings. Early identification of these elements helps parents apply focused treatments, offer suitable support, and design surroundings that encourage emotional well-being and positive conduct. Early on, understanding these causes can help you jump in with the appropriate techniques, provide the necessary support, and create an environment where they may flourish with a grin!

Navigating Behavioural Challenges: Practical Tips and Real-Life Examples

When your child acts in a way that you didn't expect, ask yourself, "What's really going on here?" There must be a reason for this behaviour, right?" A child's temper tantrum might not just be a temper tantrum; it could be a way for them to show their anger or get attention in a busy place.

To understand and help children with behaviour problems, you need to know the different psychological factors that affect their actions. Think of yourself as a bridge architect; each support beam stands for your ability to empathize with and comprehend your child's point of view. Building trust and improving communication starts with approaching behavioural challenges with empathy and exploration.

Parenting is like riding a roller coaster: ups and downs, along with occasionally surprising turns. Remember that you are not alone on this journey. Every parent struggles with behaviour; it's normal to ask for help when you need it. Reaching out shows strength rather than weakness, whether it means chatting with a friend, consulting a parenting blog, or consulting a professional.

So inhale deeply, accept the journey, and know that you have what it takes to negotiate every behavioural obstacle that arises with compassion, empathy, and a decent sense of humour.

These helpful tips can enable parents to properly control behaviour and promote good development:

Promote Emotional Regulation

Children's outbursts of emotion can be too much for them to handle, but teaching them ways to deal with them, like deep breathing or making a space to calm down with sensory toys, can help. Be calm and praise them when they try to control their feelings. This will help them stick to positive habits.

Practical strategies to promote emotional regulation:

- ✓ **Do deep breathing exercises with your child:** Teach them to take slow, deep breaths when they are angry or upset. Tell them to breathe deeply through their noses, then slowly out of their mouths. Deep breathing can help them calm their minds and bodies.

- ✓ **Set aside a calm-down corner:** Pick a spot in your home to use as a calm-down corner. To make it feel better, add soft blankets, stuffed animals, or touch toys inside. You should tell your child to use this area when they need to calm down and take a break.

✓ **Positive Self-Talk:** Teach your child how to control their feelings by saying positive things to themselves. It's beneficial to say things like "I can handle this" or "I am calm and in control." Talking positively to themselves can help them change how they think when things are hard.

✓ **Practice awareness:** Teach your child simple mindfulness techniques, like paying attention to their breathing or feeling things in their body. Mindfulness teaches children to be more aware of their feelings before acting on them.

✓ **Engage in physical activities:** Yoga, dancing, or playing outside are all beneficial examples of physical activities that can help you control your emotions. Moving around can help you get rid of worry and release pent-up energy.

✓ **Make Visual Calm-Down Tools:** Create visual tools like a "calm-down jar" (a jar filled with glitter and water that settles when shaken) or a "feelings chart" that lists different emotions and ways to deal with them. Visual aids can help younger children better understand and handle their feelings.

✓ **Be an Example of positive Behaviour:** Kids learn by watching, so show them how to be cool and control their emotions. Your example of staying calm when upset or stressed will encourage them to do so.

Chapter 4 | Understanding the Causes of Behaviour Problems

Life example:

Six-year-old Sarah regularly breaks into tears and tosses her pencils over the table when she gets annoyed with her school work. Understanding her difficulty with emotional control, her parents set aside a "calm-down corner" in her room. They stuff it with weighted blankets, soft cushions, and stress-relieving items such as squishy balls and glitter-covered sensory jars.

When Sarah gets stressed by homework, her parents gently lead her to the calm-down area. They encourage her to inhale deeply and squeeze the stress ball to alleviate tension. Sarah learns to recognise her rising emotions and deliberately chooses the calm-down zone to cool off before picking back up her homework.
At the conclusion of every effective homework session, Sarah's parents congratulate her for her successful attempts to control her emotions, especially when she manages her impatience without throwing a tantrum. They also offer a little incentive.

Respect and Understand Temperament

A child's temperament determines how they react to different stimuli. Make sure to schedule activities for quieter periods, or give your child headphones that block out background noise if they are sensitive to it. Consider their preference for stability or adaptability, and adjust your expectations accordingly.

Practical strategies to respect and understand your child's temperament:

- ✓ **Acknowledge Individual Differences:** Know that every child responds to events based on their particular temperamental nature. While some kids could adjust readily to changes in their surroundings, others might be more sensitive to sensory cues.

- ✓ **Manage or modify expectations:** Adjust your standards and parenting style based on how your child behaves. You could use noise-blocking headphones or plan trips for when it's quieter if your child is sensitive to loud noises.

- ✓ **Make a Comfortable Environment:** Give your child a safe, reliable space that fits their personality. For example, if your child likes sequences, set regular times for meals, playtime, and sleep every day.

- ✓ **Encourage Self-Expression:** Let your children be themselves and share how they feel and what they like. Be considerate of their mindset and honour their desire for alone time or companionship. For instance, make sure your child has access to peaceful areas where they may read or do other solo hobbies without interruptions.

- ✓ **Use positive reinforcement:** Praise your child for beneficial actions that fit his or her personality. When they do a competent job of handling their feelings or adapting to new scenarios, praise them.

- ✓ **Validating your child's feelings and offering comfort** when they feel overwhelmed are two ways to assist them in navigating emotional sensitivities. A child who becomes agitated easily might calm down with soothing words and personal comfort.

Chapter 4 | Understanding the Causes of Behaviour Problems

Life example:

Michael, who is seven years old, has a very sensitive disposition that makes him easily frightened by chaotic situations and loud sounds. Even though his family likes going to the amusement park, he frequently has tantrums due to the crowds and loudness. To combat this, Michael's parents schedule their trips during off-peak hours when the park is less busy.

They inform Michael of their plan before they leave for the park, describing the attractions they want to see and the rides they intend to take. Michael feels more prepared and safer because of this. In addition, they've brought his beloved teddy bear and headphones that can block out other sounds.

So that Michael can relax and recharge, they take several pauses in less busy places during the day. During these intervals, they provide him with refreshments and commend his courage and flexibility.

The family had a more peaceful trip since Michael's sensitive needs were considered during planning. Since Michael feels understood and supported, there will be fewer meltdowns and more enjoyment for everyone. As he consistently applies these tactics, Michael gains self-assurance and learns to control his sensitivity in trying situations.

Support Cognitive Challenges

Structured habits and visual tools can help children with cognitive problems, such as ADHD. Divide tasks into manageable steps and work with teachers to ensure identical methods at school and home. This method helps them stay focused and creates a positive learning environment.

Practical strategies to support cognitive challenges:

✓ **Break Tasks Down:** Break tasks down into smaller steps that you can handle. For example, if your child has trouble doing their chores, divide them up into smaller parts and let them take a short break between each one. This makes the job less stressful and helps you stay focused.

✓ **Use visual aids**, like plans, charts, and timers, to help you stay organized and keep track of time. For instance, make a picture plan of the things you need to do in the morning, like brushing your teeth, getting dressed, and eating food. A timer can help your child stay on track by giving each task a set amount of time.

✓ **Establish a structured environment** by creating a daily plan so that everyone knows what to expect. For example, make sure there is a place to do homework that isn't near any other things. Stick to the same times for food, chores, and sleep every day to promote stability and predictability.

✓ **Use positive reinforcement:** To help children make progress, reward hard work and excellent behaviour. For instance, set up a reward system where your child gets stickers or points for finishing chores or showing progress. Save these points for a small prize or a fun activity.

✓ **Give Simple, direct Instructions:** Give clear, concise instructions and make sure they are understood. Instead of telling them, "Clean your room," say things like, "Put your toys in the bin," "Make your bed," and "Put your clothes in the hamper."

✓ **Take time-outs and breaks:** Short breaks and physical movement can help you concentrate and feel less restless. If your child works hard for 20 minutes, let them take a five-minute break to move around or stretch. To help them calm down, do things like jumping jacks or go for a short walk.

✓ **Get professional help:** work with teachers, therapists, or other specialists to make personalized plans for support. For example, work with your child's teacher to make adjustments in the classroom, like giving them more time on tests or letting them choose where to sit. Talk to an occupational therapist about ways to improve your brain functions or sensory processing skills.

Life example:

David, a nine-year-old with ADHD, often struggled to complete his homework due to being easily overwhelmed. To support him, his parents broke down his tasks into smaller, manageable steps. Instead of tackling an entire math worksheet, David was asked to complete five problems at a time, with short breaks in between to stretch or play.

They also created a visual schedule with pictures for his evening routine, including homework, dinner, and bedtime. This helped David understand what to expect and gave him a sense of control.

Chapter 4 | Understanding the Causes of Behaviour Problems

> To motivate him, they introduced a reward system. David earned points for completing each set of problems, which he could trade for a treat or a special activity like extra playtime or a family game night. This approach made homework less daunting and more rewarding for David.

Address Past Trauma Sensitively

Having a traumatic event can have a big effect on how you act. To deal with past trauma in a thoughtful way, you need to make sure that children have a secure and supportive place to heal and feel safe. Reassure your child that they are safe, and slowly put them in similar situations at their own pace if they show signs of worry from things that happened in the past. Seek professional help in the form of therapy or counselling to better handle their feelings and fears.

Practical strategies to address past trauma sensitivity:

✓ **Establish a Secure Environment:** Pick out a peaceful, comforting area in the house where your child may relax and feel comfortable. If a child goes through a stressful event like a house fire, their parents may create a comforting space in their bedroom by placing cushions, a night light, and other items that help them relax. In times of worry, the little one finds solace in this secure area, where they may read a book or snuggle up with a beloved stuffed animal.

✓ **Keep to a Regular Schedule:** This will give stability and security. Parents may help their children feel safer and less anxious after experiencing traumatic events, such as a car accident, by establishing predictable routines, such as mealtimes, bedtime tales, and weekend activities.

✓ **Foster Open Communication:** Give the child a safe space to share how they're feeling and what they're thinking. Fear and uncertainty are common reactions for children who witness domestic abuse. kids have frequent one-on-one time with their parents before bed, when kids may share their feelings of the day, and their parents reassure them that it's alright to be fearful and that they are protected.

✓ **Get professional help:** Talk to a therapist or psychologist specializing in trauma. A trauma-informed counsellor may work with a child who has just survived a natural catastrophe to help them begin the healing process. The child has the opportunity to work through their feelings and build resilience via play therapy and parent-led conversations.

✓ **Gradually Reintroduce Triggers:** Carefully and supportively reintroduce triggers to a traumatized child. When a child develops a fear of water as a result of a near-drowning incident, their parents may enrol them in a gentle swim class. In this class, the child will learn to swim with the help of an instructor while beginning by sitting on the sidelines.

By changing these tactics to fit your child's specific needs and situation, you can help them grow and deal with behaviour problems in a patient and understanding way. You can help your child's growth and well-being in many ways by creating a supportive setting at home and working with teachers and other experts.

Chapter 4 | Understanding the Causes of Behaviour Problems

Life example:

Twelve-year-old Lily started to get anxious after seeing a car accident on her way home from school. Her parents set up a secure place in her bedroom with her preferred books, cosy blankets, and soothing music to help her. Lily searched for solace in this area whenever she felt overwhelmed or nervous; reading or listening to calming music helped her feel safe.

They kept regular meals and bedtimes at home, which gave Lily consistency and helped her ground herself throughout periods of more worry following the accident.

Lily's family had periodic conversations where they addressed emotions and issues to encourage honest communication. This provided Lily with a secure space to share her worries about car accidents and get comfort from her parents' attempts to guarantee her safety.

Lily went to weekly sessions to learn coping mechanisms, including deep breathing and imagery, after seeing a child psychologist focused on trauma. Over time, these strategies helped her control her fear and sort out her emotions about the accident.
Starting with short drives around the neighbourhood, Lily's parents gradually returned car rides to regulated settings. Thanks to the encouraging techniques her parents used, every good trip increased Lily's confidence and helped her get over her anxiety about riding in cars.

Foster Positive Family Dynamics

It's essential to encourage positive family relationships because they make sure that everyone feels supported and understood. This makes people feel better emotionally and makes family ties stronger. Openly sharing your thoughts and feelings is a beneficial way to improve your conversation skills. It also helps to solve problems peacefully and builds trust.

Practical strategies to foster positive family dynamics:

✓ **Make sure everyone can understand each other:** Encourage family members to express their emotions and thoughts without fear of judgment. For instance, family time provides an opportunity for everyone to express themselves and receive attention. This makes sure that everyone feels like they are important and understood.

✓ **Be Clear About the Rules and Expectations:** Make sure everyone in the family knows how to behave and what their roles are. For example, make sure everyone knows their part and how they can help the family's well-being by clearly outlining home chores and what is expected of them.

✓ **Use positive reinforcement:** Offer praise and gifts for good behaviour. Let's say a child helps a sister without being asked. To show appreciation, say something like, "I saw how helpful you were by sharing your toys with your brother." Wow, that was very kind!"

✓ **Spend quality time with your family** by planning regular activities like hiking, cooking, or playing board games that everyone can enjoy. For instance, make Sunday nights "family game night" so that everyone can play and enjoy each other's company.

Chapter 4 | Understanding the Causes of Behaviour Problems

✓ **Promote empathy and problem-solving:** Show children how to have empathy by understanding them and helping them work through problems. For example, if brothers fight over who gets to play with the toys, help them talk about how they feel without getting frustrated and come up with answers together. This will help them respect each other and work together.

Life example:

Emily, who is eleven years old, often felt left out at school because she had trouble making friends at playtime and lunch. Emily had trouble making friends, so her parents asked her classmates over for play dates and other activities from time to time. They told Emily to participate in events outside of school so she could find out more about her interests and meet other kids who liked the same things she did.

Emily slowly made friends and gained confidence in social situations during these play dates and events. Her parents also taught her how to get along with other people by having her start conversations and join in group events. Emily began to feel more included and respected among her peers as her group of friends grew and her interactions at school became more positive. Emily's parents' proactive method not only helped her get over feeling alone, but it also helped her make friends and improved her general health and well-being.

By using these tactics in your child's daily life and changing them to fit their specific needs, you can make the home a safe and caring place that helps them grow and develop. Remember that every

Chapter 4 | Understanding the Causes of Behaviour Problems

child is different, so the best way to encourage good behaviour and mental health is to adapt your approach with kindness and understanding.

Chapter 5

RECOGNISING NEURODEVELOPMENTAL DISORDERS

Let's learn more about brain disorders, which could have a big effect on your child's health and growth if you take them seriously. A wide range of problems known as neurodevelopmental disorders impact a child's ability to learn, perform appropriately, and engage socially. Remember that these disorders come in different forms, and each has its own effects and problems. Accept that everyone is different; there are a lot of different traits and abilities waiting to be found.

What are Neurodevelopmental Disorders?

Neurodevelopmental disorders are conditions that affect the brain's growth and development. This can make it challenging for a child to learn, talk, and interact with their surroundings. Neurodevelopmental disorders function similarly to improvised jazz in the brain, producing unexpected sounds and following their own rhythm. These conditions usually show up in kids early in life, when their brains are still developing. They change the way the brain works, which has an effect on how we learn, behave, and connect with others.

Types of Neurodevelopmental Disorders

- **Attention-Deficit/Hyperactivity Disorder (ADHD):** A person with ADHD has a brain that is like being on high alert, making it challenging to focus, sit still, or control their emotions. Children with ADHD may trouble focusing in class, move around a lot, or answer questions without thinking. Consider the example of a child who always forgets their homework because they have trouble focusing.

- **Autism Spectrum Disorder (ASD)**: People with ASD have trouble understanding and interacting with the world around them. It changes how people talk, act, and connect with others. It might be challenging for kids with ASD to make friends, follow social rules, or get used to changes in their habits. Imagine a child who likes to play alone and gets upset when their daily routine changes without warning.

- **Learning Disorders or Difficulties:** Learning disorders like dyslexia, dyscalculia, and dysgraphia make it hard to learn and use certain skills. For example, dyslexia makes it hard to read, and dyscalculia makes it hard to understand math. Imagine a child who reads slowly and has trouble understanding what they are reading, even though they keep trying.

- **Intellectual Disability:** This type of disability can be mild to serious and affects a person's ability to learn and solve problems. It alters normal activities such as talking to people and taking care of yourself. For instance, a child with a major brain disability might need extra help with basic things like eating or getting dressed.

- **Communication Disorders:** People with these disorders have trouble speaking, understanding words, or both. Speech sound disorders make it hard to pronounce words clearly, and language disorders make it hard to communicate clearly. Imagine a child who stutters or has trouble putting their thoughts into words that make sense.

- **Motor Disorders:** These disorders affect how well a person moves and coordinates their movements. For example, developmental coordination disorder makes it harder to do things like tie your shoelaces or catch a ball. People with Tourette syndrome make sounds and move their bodies without meaning to. These are called tics. Think about a kid who has trouble riding a bike or sitting still in class without moving around.

- **Sensory Processing Disorder (SPD):** People with SPD have trouble understanding how their brain processes sensory information, which can make them more sensitive to or confused by everyday things like sounds, sights, tastes, and smells. Children with SPD may strongly respond to certain feelings or seek other emotions very deeply. Imagine a child who covers their ears when there are loud noises or refuses to wear clothes because of how they feel.

- **Other Disorders:** Fetal alcohol spectrum disorders (caused by drinking alcohol during pregnancy), Rett syndrome (a genetic disorder that affects brain development), and selective mutism (refusing to speak in certain situations) are less common neurological disorders.

Spotting Signs and Symptoms

It is natural for parents to be concerned about how their child is growing and changing. Do you notice that your child continues to behave or act in ways that don't seem normal? Do they find it hard to do things that other kids find simple? Are there problems in social settings or feelings that come up out of nowhere? These are good questions that can help parents figure out what signs might mean that their child needs more care or an exam from a doctor.

Chapter 5 | Recognising Neurodevelopmental Disorders

Parents must be very aware of and pay close attention to a wide range of behavioural, cognitive, and social cues that may indicate their child is having problems in order to spot signs and symptoms of neurological disorders. Signs could include delays in speech and language development, trouble interacting with others, repeated habits, and difficulty paying attention and focusing. When you're a parent, trust your gut. If something seems odd, you should look into it further.

Neurodevelopmental diseases can be hard, but they can also be very rewarding. It's like having a VIP pass to a world full of different skills, ideas, and ways of looking at life's events. Dealing with cognitive disorders is a lot like dancing in the rain: it's messy and unexpected, but there are always joyful and exciting moments.

Here is a closer view of how parents could spot these indicators:

Behavioural Signs

Look for patterns of behaviour that don't seem to fit with normal growth. For example, a child with ADHD might be very active, act without thinking, and have trouble staying focused on chores. They might talk over other people a lot or have trouble waiting their turn. A child with autism spectrum disorder (ASD) may have repetitive habits, limited hobbies, and social problems like not being able to make eye contact or understand social cues.

> **Example:** Sarah, a 6-year-old, doesn't like playing with her friends at playtime and would rather line up her toys in a certain way. Breaking her routine upsets her, and she finds it challenging to engage in pretend play with other children.

Cognitive Signs

These challenges can manifest as difficulties in learning and understanding concepts. Children with learning disorders may have trouble reading, writing, or math, even if they are smart. They might have trouble remembering things, planning their work, or following directions.

> **Example:** Eight-year-old David struggles to read aloud and frequently mixes like-sounding words. He still struggles with spelling and understanding books, even with extra guidance from his teacher

Social Signs

Pay attention to your child's social interactions. Making friends, reading social signs, and keeping a conversation going are all challenges that children with neurodevelopmental problems may face. They may like to be alone or have trouble finding common ground with their classmates.

> **Example:** Ten-year-old Alex regularly takes things seriously and misinterprets humour, which causes problems with peers. He avoids social events at school and likes to play computer games by himself.

Emotional Signs

Watch how your child responds emotionally and regulates themselves.

Chapter 5 | Recognising Neurodevelopmental Disorders

Children with neurodevelopmental problems may have exaggerated emotional sensitivity, anxiety, or mood swings unrelated to their circumstances.

> **Example:** Emily, a seven-year-old, experiences intense test anxiety. She worries excessively about making mistakes and failing, frequently seeking reassurance from her parents and teachers.

Physical Signs

Although less prevalent, some neurodevelopmental problems might show physical signs. Children with motor disorders such as cerebral palsy, for example, could find coordination, balance, or fine motor abilities challenging.

> **Example:** Jack, a little boy of nine years old, has cerebral palsy and has a hard time controlling his hands, which causes him to have trouble writing and drops things often.

Key Clues for Parents:

✓ Developmental Milestones: See how your child's skills and behaviour match age-appropriate norms.

✓ Consistency: Check for behaviours that stay the same over time and in various settings.

✓ Parental Intuition: Trust your instincts. See medical professionals for direction if you worry about the growth of your child.

Seeking Professional Guidance

Never hesitate to see professionals such as developmental specialists, child psychologists, or physicians if you observe symptoms that might indicate your child may be suffering from a neurodevelopmental condition. You can rely on their expertise in child development and learning to provide you with personalized guidance and assistance. Listening to their advice early on may greatly benefit your child's success.

Supporting Your Child

Gain strength by learning as much as you can about your child's illness. Staying strong and supporting a child who is dealing with neurodevelopmental issues can be challenging. Just remember, you are not alone. Recognising your child's unique needs requires persistence, empathy, and, at times, some imagination. Every little thing counts, whether it's making their house a more peaceful place, giving them visual aids, helping them discover things they love, or getting them in touch with professionals who can cater to their specific requirements. Your unwavering commitment and affection are unparalleled resources for your child.

Love, guidance, and inspiration are essential for any child, but children with neurodevelopmental disorders may require extra support to overcome their unique obstacles. Keep going; parenting a child with a neurodevelopmental impairment isn't easy. Your efforts are significant, and they have a profound impact on your child's development and happiness. Never give up, no matter how difficult things get. You are doing a fantastic job, even on the most difficult days.

Always remember that every moment of patience and every choice made with their best interests in mind has a huge impact on their future.

> **Remember to take time for yourself, too.** Taking care of yourself and finding time to recharge are equally important to ensuring your child's well-being. Keep up the excellent work, and remember that asking for help when you need it is completely acceptable.

Chapter 6
POSITIVE PARENTING TECHNIQUES

Encouraging Independence and Responsibility

Like making sure your kids eat their veggies and brush their teeth, being a parent is more than that. Additionally, it's about helping them become mature, independent people. Now the question is: how do we develop these traits in a healthy way? Let's look at some tips, put some thought-provoking questions, and sprinkle a bit of humour in there too.

Give Them Choices

Do you feel like you're always telling your kids what to do? Instead, provide them with choices. Ask something like, "Would you rather wear the blue shirt or the red shirt today?" "Do you want broccoli or carrots?" Creating the impression of power is the whole point, right? This small change can help them feel more in charge and learn how to make choices.

- **Question to Think About:** When was the last time you let your child select something they really wanted?

- **Tip:** Give them small choices at first, and as they get older, give them bigger choices.

Set Clear Expectations

When children understand their expectations, they perform better.

Setting clear standards gives them a sense of safety and helps them know what they need to do.

- **Question to Think About:** Have you told your child exactly what you expect from them, or do you think they already know?

- **Tip:** Be clear. Say "Please put your toys away after playing" instead of "Be good."

Teach Problem-Solving Skills

Encourage your child to solve their own problems instead of fixing them for them. This makes them feel more confident and free.

- **Question to Think About:** How often do you fix things for your child instead of letting them figure it out?

- **Tip:** As soon as they tell you about a problem, ask, "What do you think we should do about this?" Like letting them figure out that puzzle with the Lego pieces—they'll get it in the end, and the victory dance will be worth it.

Assign Age-Appropriate Chores

Involving children in household tasks helps them learn about responsibility and the importance of making a contribution to the family.

- **Question to Think About:** Does your child have specific, ongoing responsibilities around the house?

- **Tip:** Take it easy at first, doing things like feeding the cat or setting the table. Congratulate them on their attempts to encourage a positive attitude. And who knows? Perhaps in the future, they'll outperform your washing skills.

Encourage Self-Help Skills

Children develop a sense of autonomy as they learn to accomplish activities on their own, such as putting on their own clothes or preparing a simple snack.

- **Question to Think About:** Are you helping your child out with something they may be learning to accomplish on their own?

- **Tip:** Demonstrate the process, then step back and give them a good go. The time invested will be well worth it.

Allow Natural Consequences

The most effective method of teaching children is to let them see the results of their own actions in the real world.

- **Question to Think About:** Do you ever try to protect your child from the consequences of their own actions?

- **Tip:** Make them deal with consequences at school if they fail to turn in their school work. The learning experience is profound.

Use Positive Reinforcement

Children may be more willing to take on more responsibility when they are praised and rewarded.

- **Question to Think About:** Are you more likely to notice when your child does something properly, or when they make a mistake?

- **Tip:** Comment particularly on their efforts, for example, you may say something like, "I saw you put your shoes away without being asked. Great job!" to express your appreciation for their efforts. Superb work!" Simply remembering to replace the toothpaste cap is an accomplishment worthy of praise; after all, we all need a little motivation now and again.

Be Patient and Consistent

Getting children to be independent and responsible takes time and care.

- **Question to Think About:** Do you always do what you say you'll do and meet your expectations?

- **Tip:** Being consistent builds trust and helps children know what to expect. Do it anyway, even if it's challenging. It's important to be consistent, but if you're trying to hide the good snacks from children, then being inconsistent is fine.

Recall that raising autonomous, responsible children is a marathon rather than a sprint. Cherish the little achievements as you go, and remember to give yourself some time. Parenting is complicated; you also deserve time off. Therefore, the next time you find yourself overwhelmed, ask yourself: When was the last time I had some time to myself?

Building Self-Esteem and Confidence

Building strong self-esteem and confidence in children is like creating a masterpiece: it needs the correct tools, time, and love. So, what's the best way to accomplish it? To keep things light-hearted, let's get into some practical advice, questions to think about, and a little bit of humour.

Praise the Effort, Not Just the Outcome

Have you ever thought about how good it feels when someone notices how hard you worked, no matter what the outcome was? Children feel the same way!

- **Question to Consider:** When was the last time you complimented your child for their effort instead of only their successes?

- **Tip:** Instead of just saying, "Great job on getting an A," say something like, "I'm proud of how hard you worked on that picture."

Encourage Trying New Things

Your child's self-esteem and ability to identify their own strengths can be enhanced by encouraging them to do new things.

- **Question to Consider:** Are your children following the same pattern or are they developing an adventurous spirit?

- **Tip:** Suggest a new activity or hobby for them. Though they're not perfect, it's about learning and developing. The delight lies in the attempt! After all, one never knows. Your child may be the next Picasso. Alternatively, children can simply love finger painting a lot.

Celebrate Small Wins

Little accomplishments might be as significant as more major ones. Celebrate those small triumphs!

- **Question to Consider:** Do you devote time to recognising and appreciating your child's minor accomplishments?

- **Tip:** Emphasize things like learning to tie their shoes or finishing a puzzle. Situations like this boost confidence. To be honest, we all need a little celebration to make Monday go without losing our keys.

Model Positive Self-Talk

The way we talk to ourselves can teach our children a lot. When you treat yourself well, they will learn to do the same.

- **Question to Consider:** How do you talk about yourself with your child? Do you want to be a role model to others?

- **Tip:** Practice positive self-talk. Say something like, "I'm getting better every day," rather than, "I'm so bad at this." Even superheroes need encouragement from time to time, so consider this a pep talk.

Foster Independence

Giving your child age-appropriate tasks can help tremendously with their confidence and sense of competence. Imagine that someday they might appreciate you for teaching them how to load the dishwasher, even if half the dishes come out still unclean. All of it is a part of the road to independence.

- **Question to Consider:** When was the last time you let your child try anything on their own — even if it meant they might fail?

- **Tip:** Start with easy chores like sorting the waste products, watering the plants, or putting away their toys. Respect their work and accomplishments. Allowing children to make mistakes fosters self-reliance. For instance, let them help with basic household chores or pack their own school bag.

Developing self-esteem and confidence in your child requires time, patience, and a great deal of love. Super parents, keep taking care of those little hearts and minds. One little step at a time, you are doing an amazing job. The key is to make them feel respected and capable in a loving environment. So the next time you're in the heart of turmoil, ask yourself: Am I fostering my child's self-esteem today?

Dealing with Tantrums and Meltdowns

Being a parent is like being on a roller coaster: thrilling, full of surprises, and never predictable. And if there's one thing that everyone goes through, it's dealing with tantrums. Imagine for a second a world where your child had the analytical mind of an experienced lawyer and the dramatic talent of a soap opera star, all bundled into one little shape.

A tantrum is like a set of fireworks: it may be both loud and dramatic, and you'll marvel at how something so little can make such a show out of it. On the bright side, you have company on this crazy journey. Tantrums are common in children, and while they can be difficult to handle, they are also an important part of a child's growth and development. Parents can help their children develop healthy emotional regulation skills by patiently and empathetically recognising and addressing the root causes.

> There are many reasons why children have temper tantrums, and knowing these can help parents understand and deal with them:

Expressing Emotions: Children's difficulties communicating their feelings verbally often lead to tantrums. Tantrums may be a means of expression for strong emotions when one feels overwhelmed, annoyed, or unable to get their way.

Seeking Attention: Sometimes, especially in cases when children feel ignored or disregarded in particular circumstances, tantrums are a means of attracting attention for them.

Testing Boundaries: Children challenge limits and boundaries as they grow to better understand their surroundings and personal individuality. Tantrums may arise when they come across restrictions they feel to be limiting.

Fatigue or Hunger: Like adults, children might get more restless and prone to emotional outbursts when they are hungry or exhausted.

Sensory Overload: Certain children are particularly sensitive to sensory cues such as noise, strong lighting, or crowded areas. Overwhelmed by sensory data, they could go into meltdowns.

Puberty: Hormonal changes brought on by puberty might cause mood swings and emotional instability that could show up as emotional outbursts or tantrums.

Social Problems: Tantrums can also be brought on by social problems, including difficulties in social contacts, such as troubles forming friends, feeling excluded from social groups, or peer pressure.

Communication Challenges: Children with speech or language difficulties may find it difficult to effectively express their wants and feelings, which may cause annoyance and outbursts.

Transition and Change: Any major change in habit, surroundings, or family dynamics — such as parents' divorce or a new house — may overwhelm children and cause them to act out.

Expectations Not Met: Children may become irritated or frustrated when their expectations about activities, rewards, or results are not met, which may escalate into a tantrum.

> Knowing how to handle a child's temper tantrums based on his or her age can help parents do the right thing. Here's a list with some examples:

Toddler tantrums (ages 1 to 3 years old): Toddlers often throw temper tantrums because they are frustrated with their inability to communicate and their growing sense of freedom. A child might have a temper tantrum if they can't say what toy they want, which could include crying and stomping their feet.

Preschooler Tantrums (ages 3 to 5): Preschoolers still have temper tantrums, but they may also do them when they're trying to figure out how to behave and follow the rules. For example, a toddler might have a temper tantrum when they are told it's time to leave the playground. They might protest loudly and refuse to go.

School-Age Tantrums (6–12 years old): Older kids may not have as many temper tantrums, but they can still have trouble controlling their feelings, especially when they are under a lot of pressure at school or with friends. A child of school age might have a temper tantrum if they get a bad grade on a test, crying or yelling to show how upset they are.

Teenage Emotional Outbursts (13–18 years old): Teenagers have emotional outbursts that can look like temper tantrums. This is usually because of changes in hormones, stress from school or relationships, and problems with who they are. To give you an example, a teenager might lose it when their bedtime is set earlier than they thought, showing anger or rebellion.

Keep in mind that having tantrums is very normal and a natural aspect of being a child. Your child will benefit greatly in life by learning important emotional skills from you, so it's important to be patient and use these tactics. Managing meltdowns and tantrums isn't easy, but here are a few methods to get through the rough patches:

Tips for Navigating Tantrums and Meltdowns:

- ✓ **Recognising Developmental Stage:** Tantrums change as children do, reflecting their changing strengths and weaknesses.

- ✓ **Stay Calm Yourself:** The best way to deal with a tornado is to remain calm. It's not easy! It is possible to de-escalate the situation by remaining cool. Relax; no matter how awful things become, you are the rock that everyone can rely on.

- ✓ **Understanding Triggers:** Consider what often triggers your child's tantrums so you can better understand their behaviour. When are they most likely to be exhausted, hungry, or angry? You can better prepare for and avoid meltdowns if you are aware of what sets them off.

- ✓ **Empathy and Validation:** Validate your child's emotions even as you establish limits; this demonstrates empathy and validation. When you say no, acknowledge their disappointment but explain gently. Hearing them out when they're upset is crucial for some children. One of the phrases to try is, "I can tell you're really distressed right now." When you use it, amazing things happen.

- ✓ **Teaching Coping Skills:** Show children how to recognise when they're feeling sad or frustrated and how to control their emotions using techniques like deep breathing, counting to ten, or just taking a short break.

- ✓ **Consistency:** One way to reduce the likelihood of tantrums is to be consistent with routines and expectations. In the case of screen time and housework, for example, set firm limits and adhere to them.

- ✓ **Role Modelling:** Demonstrate to children how to remain calm and composed in stressful situations, as well as how to solve problems effectively. The right amount of humour may do wonders for relieving stress and changing the atmosphere.

Life example of parenting approach: Understanding Triggers

Imagine Sarah, a lively four-year-old, having a tantrum whenever you ask her to put away her toys before she goes to bed. This occurs frequently when she is exhausted from a long day at preschool, as her parents have seen. They take a more peaceful attitude rather than demanding quick cleanliness. They sit down with Sarah and tell her they understand how tired she is. They then suggest that they clean up together as a game. This not only makes Sarah less resistant, but it also teaches her responsibility in a good way.

Life example of parenting approach: Consistency

Sophie, a lively four-year-old, frequently threw intense tantrums not only at bedtime but also during bath-time. Her parents noticed that any deviation from her bath-time routine often triggered these outbursts, making evenings stressful for everyone involved. Understanding the importance of consistency, Sophie's parents decided to implement a strict bath-time schedule alongside her bedtime routine. They established a structured bath-time routine that included washing, playing with bath toys, and winding down with gentle songs or stories. They ensured that bath-time occurred at the same time each evening, providing Sophie with predictability and stability in her evening routine.

Initially, Sophie resisted the new bath-time routine with tears and protests, as she preferred to continue playing. However, her parents remained firm and calmly guided her through each step of the routine, offering reassurance and support. They consistently followed the schedule, gently reminding Sophie of the routine's sequence and the importance of bath-time before bedtime. Over time, Sophie began to anticipate and accept the bath-time routine, knowing what to expect each evening. With the establishment of this consistent routine, Sophie's tantrums during bath-time significantly decreased, contributing to a more peaceful evening atmosphere for the entire family. Through their commitment to consistency, Sophie's parents effectively supported her in developing positive bedtime habits and reducing evening conflicts.

Life example of parenting approach: Understanding Triggers

Emma, who is six years old, often has temper tantrums when she has to leave the playground or put down her toys to go inside. Her parents notice that these temper tantrums get worse when she is rushed or when plans change at the last minute. Because they know Emma has trouble with changes, they start using visual timers to let her know when the game is over. In addition, they warn her in person ahead of time and include her in decision-making whenever possible. Emma's worry and temper tantrums are lessened during these tough times by giving her predictable patterns and some control over changes.

Life example of parenting approach: Teaching Coping Skills

Two-year-old Sarah frequently has outbursts when she fails to get her preferred snack. Using distraction strategies, her parents begin teaching her basic coping mechanisms. When she starts to fuss about snacks, they have a tiny toy or book on hand to keep her focused. Gradually, Sarah discovers that there are other fun things to do besides munching and that her outbursts go away once she starts to handle disappointment.

Life example of parenting approach: Teaching Coping Skills

Eight-year-old Jack becomes frustrated when he finds he cannot handle arithmetic problems. His parents recommend deep breathing exercises as a coping mechanism. Jack's parents help him count to five and inhale deeply when he feels overwhelmed before attempting again. Jack grows more confident over time in managing his feelings and doing difficult chores without throwing fits.

Life example of parenting approach: Stay Calm Yourself

Ten-year-old Emily periodically has meltdowns when faced with difficult homework tasks. Her father, John, keeps cool by inhaling deeply and acting patiently. Instead of reacting impulsively, he gives Emily space to calm down while gently offering assistance.

"I understand how frustrating this is, but I'm confident we can find a way to overcome it," John says with empathy. By maintaining his composure, he helps Emily control her emotions and concentrate on finding solutions. Emily gradually gains the ability to stay positive through challenges and ask for assistance when she needs it.

I understand how difficult it is to maintain control during a tantrum, but please do your best. Keep in mind that, no matter how many tantrums your child has, you are always there to support them. Your child will always see you as an oasis of security, no matter how rough things get. Being a parent during a tantrum is like walking on a tightrope, but I can assure you, you're doing great. No matter how crazy things become, your child will always appreciate your patience and presence.

Life example of parenting approach: Empathy and Validation

Four-year-old James asks his parents if he can have the colourful toy truck he finds so exciting in the store. James starts to cry as they softly explain that they cannot afford it today because of financial restrictions. Knowing how disappointed he was, his parents went down to his level and said, "We see how much you like that truck." Instead, they advise that they take a picture for his wish list, acknowledging his emotions without giving in to them.

James is still sad, but his parents help him to feel acknowledged and validated. They help him understand that disappointment is common and gently and compassionately redirect his attention to other activities. Through empathy and affirmation, James learns how to control disappointment and improve their relationship. It also motivates him to be honest about his emotions and believe that his parents pay attention and listen to him.

Chapter 7
CONCLUSION

Encouragement for Parents

As we come to the end of our journey through understanding child behaviour, recognising behaviour problems, digging into their causes, and learning about good parenting skills, one thing is clear: parenting is an adventure, full of challenges but also of rewards.

Perfection isn't necessary to be a good parent; what matters is love and perseverance. Embrace the little wins, grow from the mistakes, and hold on to the special moments. You have the power to shape a future that is full of potential and hope.

Keep in mind that you are not alone as you navigate the challenges of parenthood. Despite difficulties, you and your child can always learn from them and develop. Enjoy every second of it, because your hard work will pay off in the end.

Remember that every child is different and that no one-size-fits-all parenting strategy exists as you consider the insights acquired. Trust in your ability to change and flourish with your child, so embrace the road with resiliency and will.

Emphasize the need for self-care among the responsibilities of parenthood. Spending time for yourself not only helps you to revive your spirit, but it also shows your child good conduct. Recall that you are most successful when you give your health top priority.

Chapter 7 | Conclusion

Appreciate the development you have together as a family. These achievements — a fresh awareness of your child's needs or a breakthrough in communication — are evidence of your love and dedication.

Ask others for help: friends, relatives, or parenting groups anywhere. Advice and sharing of experiences may offer priceless viewpoints and comfort in difficult situations. Ask yourself, when you feel overwhelmed: "What would a little act of self-care look like right now?" Then "Who can I reach out to for support, even just to talk?"

A lifesaver is often finding the good in the bad. Ask yourself: What entertaining story can you tell about how crazy today was? Which trait do you admire most in your child? What's one small thing you're proud of today? Can you take a moment today to realize how unique your child is?

Remember that you are not alone in the chaos when parenting feels more like managing a hectic schedule than guiding children. Any one of us has been there. The most memorable stories frequently emerge from the most chaotic days, so try to enjoy them and find humour in the chaos. Bring laughter into your parenting approach. Laughter is actually a medicine that works in times of difficulty or when you're wondering, "Why did they do that?" Laughter is the only response sometimes!

Now inhale deeply, rely on your gut feeling, and know you are doing an amazing job. In the lives of your children, you are the most significant. Keep strong, keep hopeful, and never undervalue the power of your love and commitment.

Let's continue working together to make the world a place where every child feels heard, cared for, and understood.

Dear Reader,

Thank you so much for choosing to read **Empowered Parenting: How to Manage Challenging Behaviour!** I hope you enjoyed it. Your feedback means a lot to me, and I'd love to hear your thoughts.

Could you take a moment to leave a review on Amazon? Reviews play a crucial role in helping other readers discover my book. It only takes a few minutes, and your feedback would be greatly appreciated.

Thank you once again for your support.

Warm regards,
Maryna Repei

Printed in Great Britain
by Amazon